INTRODUCTION TO

Physical Anthropology and Archaeology

Charles A. Weitz

Temple University